Playing like Timothy

written by
Johannes Waldner

illustrated by
Victor Kleinsasser

2023

Published in Canada by

Box 40 • MacGregor, MB • R0H 0R0 • Canada
P. 204–272–5132 • F. 204–252–2381

The publisher gratefully acknowledges editors
Dora Maendel, Elma Schemenauer and Donna Gamache.

MANITOBA ARTS COUNCIL
CONSEIL DES ARTS DU MANITOBA

Published with generous support from the Manitoba Arts Council.

Cover design: Yvonne Parks

ISBN: 978-0-9865381-4-8

Library and Archives Canada Cataloguing in Publication

Waldner, Johannes, 1987-
Playing like Timothy / Johannes Waldner, Victor Kleinsasser.

ISBN 978-0-9865381-4-8

I. Kleinsasser, Victor, 1970- II. Title.

PS8645.A4575P53 2011 jC813'.6 C2010-907629-X

for Mom and Dad

“Did you see how I flipped the puck right through Anthony’s legs?” Lance brags on the way to *Nochplig*. “I tied the score—four all.”

“Hey,” Anthony, the defenseman, snaps back, “that’s nothing compared to the three times I stopped you cold.”

Soon almost all the boys are boasting about plays and goals from the afternoon’s game—all except for Timothy who plays goalie. He wishes the *Mandeln* would talk about something else.

“Well,” says Anthony, “the one-glove save I made on Lance’s slap shot was the best. Man, that hurt.”

“Big deal,” says Lance. “I let you catch that one. My other easy-cheesy shots went past you like nothing.”

“Yeah,” Zack joins in, “they went past you so fast I thought you were Timothy trying to stop my shots.”

Everyone laughs, including Timothy, but inside he’s angry at Zack’s insult. He doesn’t want to show how much it hurts. “I try so hard!” he thinks to himself. “Why can’t I stop even one measly, lousy, stinking puck?”

After supper he sneaks away from the other boys. “I love hockey as much as my friends do,” he says to himself. “I love to talk about it and watch it and look at pictures of it and play it, just like they all do. But when I tell people that I’m a goalie I feel like I’m lying. I stink at it. No matter what I try, the puck still ends up in the back of the net.”

Timothy thinks of all the things he’s tried. He’s tried lying on his belly to stop the puck and he’s tried using his mitt to catch the puck. He’s tried using his skates, and he’s tried using his stick. But somehow, no matter what, the puck still goes in.

Many times he's been so frustrated that he's left the game, yelling, "I hate hockey. I'm never coming back."

His friends always coax him back with, "We'll go easy on you today." Or they say, "We'll let you pick whoever you want for your team."

Until now, he's always let them coax him back, but after what Zack said at supper, Timothy thinks he might quit forever. "It hurts too much," he says to himself heading for the house.

"What's the matter, Timothy?" his mother asks as he stomps up the front steps.

"Nothin' much," Timothy mumbles.

"That's no answer." Mom sounds worried. "Timmy, what's the problem?"

"Nothing." Timothy goes inside and slams the door behind him.

The next day, when Timothy gets home after *Mittogessn*, Mom catches him before he can sneak into his room.

"Timothy," his mom says, "if you don't tell me what the problem is, you're not getting *reascha Zwiboch* with cheese for a snack today." Mom is serious but he tries to shrug off her threat.

"Oh…hi, Mom, how was your morning?" he asks instead, with a forced smile.

Mom doesn't smile back.

Timothy looks down at his dirty socks, mumbling, "I dunno."

"Oh, yes, you know, *Liebs*." Mom reaches over, giving him a hug.

"I can't stop the puck when I'm goalie," Timothy finally says. "No matter what I do, the other *Mandlen* still score. I hate that stupid game. I'd like to take it and flush it!"

"Timothy, you know as well as I do that hockey is your best sport," Mom says in a soothing voice. "I think I know what we could do to solve this problem. I'll tell you what, you go to school now. After school, once you've had your snack, the two of us will make a secret plan to find out why you can't stop those pucks."

Timothy looks at her with surprise, but he is curious.

"Now don't tell anyone," she reminds him, as he leaves again for school.

FGHIJKLMNOPQRSTUVWXYZ
15 + 49
50 14
64
15
49

That whole afternoon Timothy can scarcely take his eyes off the clock. His *Bauch* is almost bursting with curiosity about his mom's plan.

Finally the clock shows three o'clock. It's time to do his sweeping job and run home. Quickly he cleans the hall and the coatroom, says goodbye to his teacher, Mr. Friesen, and runs out the door.

"Mom, I'm home!" Timothy yells as soon as he gets back from school.

"Hello, dear," Mom greets him with a smile, pours him a cup of tea and brings a plate of *reascha Zwiboch*.

"So, you can't stop any pucks when you're playing goalie?" she asks while Timothy is eating.

"Noooo," he groans and drops his crisp bun on the table.

"How about we practice in the hall downstairs?"

"In the hall?"

"Finish your snack and we'll go take a look."

Timothy recognizes his mom's hiding-a-secret smile.

When he gets downstairs he can't believe his eyes. A hockey net is set up in the hall, waiting for him. Several tennis balls are sitting there, too.

"Cool!" he yells, forgetting to use his inside voice. "Now I'll be able to play hockey all year round."

"Go put on your goalie gear, and I'll take some practice shots at you," Mom says.

"You—take shots on me?" Timothy laughs at the idea of her playing hockey.

"Huff-a-duff," chuckles Mom. "Yes, I can take shots on you. Just wait and see. Growing up in Snowview, I used to play with my brothers behind the hog barn."

EGGS
BANANAS
BOOM
JS

Mom's first shot sails over Timothy's shoulder into the top right corner. The second shot flies between his legs and hits the wall behind him with a thump. The third shot slides in beside his padded leg.

In fact, her first six shots *all* end up in the net behind him. Timothy never comes close to stopping even one of them.

"Hmm," his mom says to herself.

On her next shot, she takes a mighty wind-up, swinging her stick high in the air. Mom sweeps the stick down hard but misses the ball.

Timothy drops on his knees to stop it, but when he turns around to pull the ball out of the net, it's not there. He looks back to find out why, and realizes Mom had not even shot it. The ball is still waiting innocently at her feet.

“Timmy, I know what your problem is!” Mom cries.

“I need new pads?” Timothy guesses.

“No,” Mom says with a laugh. “It’s not that. It’s because you close your eyes when I shoot.”

“You mean my eyes shouldn’t be closed?”

“Of course not,” his mom says with a small smile.

“But it’s impossible to keep them open,” Timothy counters. “I can’t stand watching anyone shoot the puck at me.”

“All it takes is practice. Let’s try something. This time I’ll shoot slowly, and keep the ball on the floor. Don’t try to stop it; just watch it, and don’t close your eyes.”

They do this a few times so Timothy can practice keeping his eyes open.

“Now,” Mom says, tapping the stick on the floor, “get ready and try to stop some shots.”

13 DOZ.
EGGS

“Wow!” exclaims Timothy two shots later. “I almost got that one.

On the third try, he finally stops a shot.

“There you go!” Mom cheers. She looks almost as happy as he is. Timothy’s smile is so big he can’t talk, but his mom keeps taking shots, and he stops most of them.

After a while she starts shooting a little faster, but Timothy manages to keep his eyes open, and the balls out of the net. When Mom starts taking high shots, he misses a few, but before long he catches almost all those, too.

“It’ll come with practice,” Mom tells him. “As long as you can keep your eyes open.”

“I can’t wait to play with the *Mandlen* tomorrow,” Timothy says when they quit. “I’ll bet they’ll be surprised.”

“Show them how it’s done, Timmy,” Mom says.

The next day at the hockey rink, Lance comes in against Timothy on a breakaway. “I’ll score for sure!” he yells back to his team.

He winds up for a hard shot.

“Keep your eyes open,” Timothy tells himself as Lance winds up for the shot. “Keep your eyes open.”

The shot sails in toward Timothy. He moves his foot and *kaaa-toook*. The puck bounces off Timothy's pad. Zack's mouth is hanging open as he turns and chases the rebound.

"Yaaay! Nice save!" Timothy's teammates yell from the other side of the rink.

That game, Timothy stops many shots. Only one top-corner wrist-shot from Lance gets past him.

“Ti-mo-thy! Ti-mo-thy!” his team chants when they win the game 4–1. It’s his very first win.

“What happened to you, Timothy?” the boys ask after the game, crowding around him. “Suddenly you’re a pretty good goalie.”

Before he answers, Timothy looks up and sees Mom and Dad standing beside the rink, both smiling. They have watched him win his first game.

Timothy looks back and laughs at the boys' questions. "Wouldn't you just love to know?"

He turns and gives his mother a big grin.

Glossary

Nochplig - Supper

Mandlen - young boys up to age 15; singular: *Mandl*

Mittogessn - lunch; noon-time meal

reascha Zwiboch - roasted buns; a favourite Hutterite snack/comfort food

Liebs - Dear one; an endearment

Bauch - Stomach

Essnschuel - Children's dining room

www.ingramcontent.com/pod-product-compliance
Ingram Content Group UK Ltd.
Pitfield, Milton Keynes, MK11 3LW, UK
UKHW061952290726
14090UKWH00021B/1194